100
ANSWERS
TO THE MOST
UNCOMMON 100
QUESTIONS

By
ELIJAH MUHAMMAD
(Messenger of Allah)

Compiled & Edited
By
Nasir Makr Hakim

A
Secretarius MEMPS Publication

Acknowledgment

100 Answers To The Most
Uncommon 100 Questions

Copyright © 1992
First Edition 1992
Second Edition 1995
Revised Third Edition 2012

ISBN 13: 978-1-884855-09-2
ISBN#10: 1-884855-09-1

Published by
Secretarius MEMPS Publications
111 E Dunlap Ave, Ste 1-217 ● Phoenix, AZ 85020
Phone & Fax (602) 466-7347
Email: secmemps@gmail.com
www.memps.com

PRINTED IN THE UNITED STATES OF AMERICA

Acknowledgment

We seek the assistance of Allah (God), Who came in the Person of Master Fard Muhammad, through His Last and Greatest Messenger, the Most Honorable Elijah Muhammad.

We can never thank them enough for the Supreme Wisdom which has been showered upon us, and as the Messenger himself stated, "He (Allah) gave it to me like a flowing spring or flowing fountain. The fountain has enough drink in it to give everyone drink who come to drink."

"YOU DON'T NEED A NEW FOUNTAIN, JUST TRY AND DRINK UP WHAT THIS FOUNTAIN HAS."

Therefore, we avail ourselves of that water without hesitation, because we never get full. This means that the need for another fountain is totally obsolete.

I would like to thank the Hakim family, Rose, Dur're, Taqqee, Junaid and Khalfani, also Brother Azzam Waathiq Basit for their hard work contributed to make this work of the Messenger accessible to our people. May Allah, Master Fard Muhammad, continue to bless our continued efforts and labor.

As-Salaam-Alaikum
Nasir M. Hakim, Founder SECRETARIUS MEMPS

Introduction

In the reality we live, we are forever confronted with new experiences the forces us to rethink previously held positions on life and the factors that control it.

From the time of infancy, we learn, then relearn, what we had to that point become comfortable with. Getting comfortable sometimes makes us complacent and resistant to "another change." However, if we are fortunate or blessed, if you will, we learn that we are forever evolving and our learning process is essentially based on building on top of each thing we learn. It is an accumulative process: one block on top of another.

This can be beautifully illustrated with mathematics. We first learn numbers, their value and then their relationship with each other, to eventually their usage and function in our lives.

My intent here is not to give an elementary lesson in math, per se, but to make the point that if a wise teacher encounters you in their midst, one of the first thing that takes place is the assessment of your learning level. In other words, where are you in your development? It is pointless to interact with you using long division when you are not familiar with addition or multiplication. Why offer you meat when you have no teeth? You must give the baby milk before you give them meat.

Although this point may seem trivial to some, yet it is very profound and noteworthy to someone who is for all practical purposes, dead to the knowledge of themselves and more importantly, do not know that they are dead, because no one took the time to teach them what life is as a man or woman.

We all come here on a base or animal level until we are civilized.   Civilization is the only thing that separates us from the animals in the fields and jungles. When you don't have a proper knowledge of what you are (human) and what's expected, required or possible, then living a beast life may be normal for you.

Normal could mean being accidently or promiscuously conceived, born and registered with a birth certificate and social security number for global trading, nursed on synthetic poison like Similac, Enfamil or at best cow's milk, inducted into the government's Head-start indoctrination program that's design to break any bond with the "kid's" mother, and prepared to be another beast of burden until your health completely fails. By then, however, it is calculated that you too will have a kid that is *"accidently or promiscuously conceived, born and registered with a birth certificate and social security number for global trading ...."* The vicious cycle continues indefinitely - or does it. It doesn't have to.

At the beginning of this introduction I started by saying that, "In the reality we live, we are forever confronted with new experiences that forces us to rethink previously held positions on life and the factors that control it."

Many "truths" we cling to depend greatly on our own point of view. Our "view" has been based largely on what we got from our parents, siblings, school, closed fraternal societies, religious institutions, organizations, friends, or the streets.

Our "view" has been contrived or manufactured from many people with varying points of view that, at best, conflict on a good day.

God set forth a parable: Two men, one wholly devoted to one man, the other belonging to partners, differing. Are the two alike in condition?

They absolutely could not be.

One man or woman is focused and the other is living a life in constant conflict. We in no way are trying to force an opinion on you, beg for acceptance or trick you into accepting our view. At this stage in time and point of the resurrection and redemption process, willing souls are sought. If you can "see" or "discern" what's being offered to you and you respond accordingly, blessed are you. God, His Messenger or those who believe and follow them are not cheap.

The answers and questions contained in this book is just a glimpse into the Mind of the Creator, Who has made Himself known, because for thousands of years the people have not understood how to 'KNOW" the Creator, or God as we call Him, but worshipped their own ideas of who or what they either hoped God was or whatever they made Him out to be. It is time to come out of the darkness of confusion.   The Messenger said this in his Best Selling book, **Message To The Blackman In America** that, "As we near the exhaustion of the Wisdom of this world which has not been able to shed enough light on our path in search for that Supreme Wisdom to keep us from stumbling and falling, we now seek the Wisdom of Allah, The Best Knower and Guide in the Person of Master Fard Muhammad (to Whom be praised forever).   The reader will find that light in this book."

The Messenger once stated to his Ministers, "We are building a new world. I have to follow close to my Lord. You have to follow close to me to follow Him." This helps us to better understand just how important the Messenger's words are.   The Messenger further states, "It is so essential that you follow the Messenger, because if you do as I say you become a different person. The closer you try to live to me and try to follow me, the better your life."

When we observe the degree of confusion abounding in the lives of many who profess to be followers of the Messenger, it forces us to question, that either the teachings are a fraud and they ARE NOT, or they (lip professors) are not putting into practice that which is coming out of their mouths.

The state of affairs speak for themselves, which is why we believe that if one carries what the Messenger instructs into practice, they will get what's promised to them.   To that end, we offer these uncommonly asked questions and answers in an effort to provide the reader with a deeper insight as to what the Honorable Elijah Muhammad instructs and advises.

Allah, Master Fard Muhammad, has raised up from among us the Honorable Elijah Muhammad as our source of the truth, and the source is sufficient.

For in this day of abounding confusion among the common man and the shepherds, we were not left without guidance. The Messenger's words, instructions and advice still and always will have power, because it is from the Lord of the Worlds. To pick it up and use it, is to experience this for yourself.

The separation of the goats from the sheep was fairly easy to see after Allah's Messenger opened our eyes; yet, we had to wait on time and conditions to see the separation between the wheat and the tare; now, however, a more finer and undetectable separation is taking place and it is considered so fine and deceptive, that it is styled in scripture as a separation of the cattle from the cattle. For in this time, common sense is not good enough. Because the common man is in trouble, the common professors of Islam are in trouble and are in need of the Messenger's teachings and only the Messenger's teachings. The Messenger have said on numerous occasions that he would give $10,000 dollars out of his brother's vest pocket if anyone could find one word that he was teaching to be other than truth, as well, he offered the Pope of Rome the same and even more (per hour) if he could do so. What am I getting at?

If the Messenger was that confident over a word, how important is a word. The Messenger tells you and I that, "One wrong word can put you in the fisher's net." Would it then be safe to say that the right ones will keep you out?

These questions and answers, like all of the Messenger's teachings, are profound and must be cherished if we want life, and the Messenger as well said, to neglect them is our death.

As-Salaam-Alaikum

Minister Nasir Hakim
Founder, Secretarius MEMPS

Table of Content

Table of Content

In The Beginning

The First God

Question: Why don't we know the actual time of the beginning of the first God?

Messenger: Because there was no one there to record it. He is the God. There is no God in the Sun before you. The Blackman has no beginning.[1]

Origin of The Atom

Question: If man originated from an atom, where did the atom come from?

Messenger: It originated from space. It was out of space where he originated and the atom of life was in the darkness of the space and he came out of the atom which was in space.

Question: (by Messenger) Now you may wonder, how did that atom get in space?

Messenger: The history of the space teaches us that at that time it was nothing but darkness. If it had been light there to use our glasses on it to find out where there was an atom of life in it, before the atom was exploited to show what it was, we would tell you so, but we can't go that far with you. We don't know how the atom became in space and what came out of space a human being, that's as

---

[1] Theology of Time Audio, June 11, 1972

far back as we can go with you. This is what Allah taught me.

Question: (by Messenger) He said to me in answer to my question on man's creation:

Saviour: He said, "Brother we know that he was created, but when, we can't tell you, because we had nothing to go by. And so, He had to tell all of Himself, after He Created Himself, then we go from what He said, and I thought that that was good truth for me to teach you.[2]

Where Animals Came From

Question: Where did the lower forms of animal life come from, and how it came about?

Messenger: The form of animal life, I asked him about it, and how did they come here. The first thing He answered is every since we had the earth we had the animals on it. I said, "how was they made," He said, "I told you. Ever since we had the earth we had animals right on it."[3]

There Is Nothing Impossible

This is a reply by The Honorable Elijah Muhammad on a subject that bad been brought up about the possible and the impossible at a Table Talk of Muhammad, December 1972). Unless stated otherwise, the answers to all the following

---

[2] Theology of Time Audio, October 15, 1972
[3] Ibid.

questions, [as with this entire book], are provided by the Honorable Elijah Muhammad.

Messenger: There is nothing impossible so Allah told me. I questioned Him on this. Now, what makes the God so sure that nothing is impossible? Because if we say anything, [whether it's] this or that, is impossible, [and] we yet find ourselves within the circle of something, how can it be impossible to produce, take away or to change anything? It can't be impossible, because you may think something is impossible or don't see the possibility existing there somewhere, God can still say there is no impossibility. Here is the point He takes. Once upon a time nothing existed. You and I couldn't be sitting here discussing this because we came from nothing. So, if we were made out of nothing into something then that does away with the impossible. There can't be the impossible, because here we are ourselves produced out of nothing. That's very beautiful and a good answer.

Just like people argue with you about who is God and say that man can't be God. That's a foolish man talking like that. You can't replace man. If man is not God, then try and replace him. You can't replace him, so that's a proof right there that he's God. Your mind doesn't exceed the limitation of the First Man who is God, because He came down through us. We have been experimenting from ourselves. Everything that we think is necessary. We then can produce it and bring it into reality. If this house is sitting in my mind, but not yet built, I can bring it out of my mind into reality. That's the God.

Question: That's right, He creates it.

Messenger: That's right. You can create the image that is in you; that is in your mind once you can conceive out the image of it [or] of what you want. You then can bring it into being. That which you can't create in your mind is something you can't [create] or do. [Yet], that does not mean that it (that which you have not yet conceived of) is not coming in. It may come in your son's mind or your son's son's mind. That same thing which you were trying to get a hold of, it will come up in somebody else [mind]; that is, if it is necessary [or] if it is good.

[A good example is] our Saviour. The people had been wanting someone to conquer this devil for a long time, so [the idea] kept on going from one [mind] to another then finally His father (Allah) produced the thing that was necessary. That is a son that would be wise enough to destroy the devil. He was lucky to have been the father. Wherever there is a line for something, it will be produced.

Just like the devil wanted to learn how to fly, he kept trying some contraptions until he learned how to get up there in something heavier than air and went on to make the air his servant. It was the same thing when he was on the other side of the ocean. He kept on looking over the vast ocean and couldn't see any end to it. He wanted to see where the Sun was going down on the other side of it, so he kept on until he mastered the waves and the storms until he got over there.[4]

---

4 Table Talks of Muhammad, December 1972

The Tribe of Shabazz

Question: One of the points the Eastern Muslims remark on is that, the Qur'an says that, "He (Allah) neither begets nor is He begotten." Yet, we know that Allah came out of the family of the Tribe of Shabazz, out of the family of The God, and the God is always produced out of a fairly consistent family. From the ranks of this family, we look for the production of a God so that eventually this family actually begets the God. Knowing the Qur'an is true and that what the wise men wrote they meant, even if we don't have an understanding of it, how do we account for this apparent contradiction?

Messenger: Well, that has two meanings: There was no Tribe of Shabazz with that first God, brother. There wasn't even a tribe. Tribe means many or the head of many. So in the beginning of the Creation of the Life Germ of man, there was no Tribe. That was One God talking there; the Tribes came later. Just like the space was not full   of stars when this was going on, but now it's full. We had no Sun in that time, but now we have one around these live eggs that we call planets. We now have a Sun to keep them warm.[5]

Allah Neither Begets Nor Is He Begotten

Now, He begets not nor is He begotten, this is the theme. When was He not begotten? When had He not beget nor begotten? What do you mean, 'He

---

[5] Ibid.

begets not nor is He begotten? Is He one who does not beget Civilization when He is out of Civilization? Is He one that was not begotten by Civilization and that now the proof is He was not begotten Himself? You see this goes into a very deep science. This is what I whipped one of the Ahmadiyyah Muslims with. He used to be over here on 46th and Wabash (Chicago) at that time. We had what you might call a showdown. He wanted a showdown with me when we were on 43rd Street, so I gave it to him one Monday.

This was his subject that he picked and it also was my subject. We both had the same subject: "Say He (Allah) is One. Allah is He of Whom nothing is independent. He begets not nor is He begotten." The main question in it, with which he was trying to condemn me, was where it says, "and there is none like Him". Well, I knew this would probably be the only thing in the Qur'an he would contend with me [with], that Allah was not man, and I was proving that God was man. I showed him up by proving he didn't understand what he had taken for his defense [and] how it didn't defend him when he was trying to make it serve something other than a man.

I started off with him on the actual noun and pronoun that was used there; that it applies to "something" and not to "nothing." A spirit can't be a noun and a pronoun [and] is not something [in and] of itself. It is something that is emitted by something. You don't have steam coming out of the kettle all by itself. You've got to have something in that kettle for it to be producing steam. The steam is the energy of what you have in there. Well, anyway I won; I can tell you that.

He came down with about 7 or 8 volumes of books. I had one book, the Qur'an. I never did let him get away from the one book. I held him there, because the Qur'an is the chief of all the other books.

He and I wrestled there and we had a temple full. It was really something to see how the wisdom of Allah, as taught to me, stands up against anything you can go out there and scrape up brother. What made him so dissatisfied and confused was [that] this was their book. So, he jumped in there and told me not to dispute it from the beginning. He said, "This Qur'an, every Muslim on the earth believes it. If you don't believe in THIS Qur'an, no Muslim in Asia or any place else will like you."
I said, well I would be the same if I were them. I said, if they didn't like this Qur'an, I wouldn't like them. And he was surprised, because he thought I was going to argue the Qur'an as an untrue book. Then I said, here the Qur'an comes after the Bible and not before the Bible. It is a book produced after the Bible and given to Muhammad, but it is a book that verifies the truth of the Bible and the truth of the Bible verifies the truth of the Qur'an and it teaches you that. This he did not try to condemn. He said, "that's right, absolutely true." I said, but we must understand it. And the Bible teaches the same, we must understand. Therefore, the Holy Qur'an is not a book made whereby the average reader can read and understand it; he has to learn what it means. If he did then the prayer for

an interpreter from Abraham and Ishmael would not have been made.

The Holy Qur'an often mentions the disbeliever as not understanding. I said, what we call the creed there, "Say He Allah is One God," that's right. I said in the very beginning, He was One. He was before all and from Him we all came, right? He said, "yes!" I said, alright then, that is final and that is conclusive that we must believe that, because we all didn't come at once. 'Say He is One God and there is no God but Him." I said, this I agree 1000%.

I said, but now, He comes here and He says. "Allah is One, He begets not nor is He begotten." I said, but this can't go now back to that one in the beginning, because if that were so, how did we get here if He didn't produce us? He was not begotten, but now we're here from His creation. He created us. Well, if we were created by Him, we are begotten of Him. He gave birth to us. I said, but brother, you have to understand what this is referring to. We couldn't use this as saying He begets not nor is He begotten. We can say He is not begotten, because He was the first and if He was the first, we cannot refer to Him as being begotten for if we did, then we would have to say that one who begot Him would be the God.

So, in that sense, the "He begets not nor is He begotten" is true, but the Qur'an is a book made to [also] condemn the Trinity of Gods and this is what it is referring to. We are to get away from believing Christian beliefs and interpretations of the God.

They say there are three Gods. Well, I say if there are three, then here is a begetting and a begotten and we must make a distinction. Who was the first one? The Christians make the three equal, so now, the Qur'an has to shed the light of truth on the God, that the God is not three Gods, but is only One God and He has in the Qur'an here, He is not a Begetter. This is [referring] to the Trinity making Gods begetting God here, you see? Therefore, this must be stamped out along with the worship of a trinity of Gods.

Our god is referred to throughout the Holy Qur'an as being One God. Your Lord is One Lord it says: "Your Lord is One God." This is to condemn the teaching of that in which the showdown of truth has come; that is, a world that is teaching that the God is three. Here now, I'm saying to you that God is only One God. He is not three. He doesn't beget nor is He begotten.

You say (the Christians) that He begot Jesus for a Son. He didn't do that. The power is in the Jesus to beget, if you understand it rightly.[6]

Question: Where is Allah (God) in the Person of Master Fard Muhammad "today?"

Messenger: He Is where He Is.[7]

---

[6] Ibid.
[7] Theology of Time Audio, October 15, 1972

Elijah Muhammad:
Messenger of Allah (God)

Conversations With God

Question: Did you yourself speak to God?

Messenger: Yes, I thought I was speaking to him every since I was born, but I didn't know him. I was blinded to the knowledge of him, so He came to me and made Himself known to me. This is the way I got to Him. I was trying to see Him, but I wasn't able to approach the right path to get to Him, because I was blind when I was born by the enemy.[8]

Messenger Knows God's Voice

Question: I would like to ask a religious question. Do you have visions?

Messenger: I do not say really have visions, but I do have voices, at times.

Question: Under what conditions does that occur, when you seek it to happen?

Messenger: That comes when I am not, say, really confining myself to expect something like that or seeking something like that. That just comes, just so.

---

[8] Ibid.

Question: Do you see this as the Voice of a Spiritual Teacher, or the Voice of God?

Messenger: I know God. I was with Him about three years and about four or five months. I know His Voice. And when He Speaks, I know it.[9]

Living With God In Person

Question: The Person you refer to as living with God for three years and three or four months...?

Messenger: I am talking about the Person that Is God, and I myself, was with Him for three years and four or five months...It began in 1931. I was able to recognized Him by His Help and by the help of Scripture.

Question: Are you talking about Mr. Fard?

Messenger: It was Him that I have learned all that I am now teaching. I do not know anything of myself. It is what He Has Given me.

Question: Is it His Voice that you hear in visions now?

Messenger: It is the Same Voice. In the past and at present, I have not had to go into such things as fasting and praying that I hear Him, it is just so. Just like something happens all of a sudden out of a blue sky, like thunder.

---

[9] Elijah Muhammad Meets The Press, January 14, 1972

Question: How is it timed; every so often?

Messenger: No, it is not timed like that. It happens whenever He Gets Ready for that.

Question: Can you give me some idea?

Messenger: Whenever the time is necessary that He Speak to me. How often that takes place? I do not keep a record of it.

Question: All these 40 years, this goes on periodically?

Messenger: Yes, I have had Him Speaking to me in my ears now, in Person yes.
 There does not pass a year, that I do not Hear His Voice some time in that year.

Question: Would it be possible for you to tell us what He Has Told you in the past year, or this year?

Messenger: No, I am not here to tell you what He Said to me, yesterday, as much, unless it concerns you and the time.[10]

Master Fard Was No Drug Addict

Question: Mr. Muhammad, I'd like to know, I read in the Sun Times that Master Fard was a drug addict, is that true?

---

[10] Ibid.

Messenger: I don't think you have found any drugs here for sale have you? He didn't teach us to use drugs; that would put us out of our natural mind. In fact about it, He didn't teach us to use drugs of no kind. We use drugs sometimes due to our weakness of causing our bodies to need some kind of [nursing] of that which is now making us sick, but He didn't teach me that. He told me and taught me how to live to keep me from using anything like drugs, but sometimes we get away and we go and do that against the nature of our bodies in which they were made, then we go and look for something to help us to get back into the well being [so] we grab at anything that will give us easement [such as] drugs. But if you live like He taught me for us to live, we don't need drugs at no time. [If] we eat once every two or three days we won't need [any] drugs. You say, "Well Muhammad, they tell me you used some drugs." Yes, because I was other than myself. I wasn't eating like He told me; therefore, falling away from the way I was taught, I suffered the consequence. I suppose to pay if I don't live according to His teachings. But I was to prove it.

I could not be able to teach you if I don't taste the same as you taste. As the Bible teaches you, "In all of their afflictions he was afflicted, but yet the pleasure of the Lord will be upon him." It doesn't mean, by no means, that he was guilty of something and God afflicted him. It doesn't mean that.[11]

Question: How is your health?

---

[11] Theology of Time Audio, October 15, 1972

Messenger: My health? Well, I do very well, I think, if it Pleases Allah. And, all of the afflictions of the former Messengers, to classify Elijah that is coming just before the Great and Dreadful day of God, he must have a taste of all of it.[12]

Question: One **Question:** How old are you now?

Messenger: I am three score, ten, and three; I am 73 years old.

Question: How is your health?

Messenger: Well, as I just said a while ago all the afflictions of the other fellows (Prophets) I have to go through.

Question: When is your birthday?

Messenger: I do not know exactly my birthday. I just know the month it came in (October). So when October passes, I say I am so old and so old.[13]

I Do Not Play Games

Question: What do you do for recreation? Do you play chess?

Messenger: No, I do not play any games of chance. No, I do not ever have any time to do anything but teach and instruct Laborers how to go about their Labor.

---

[12] Elijah Muhammad Meets The Press, January 14, 1972
[13] Ibid.

Question: How long is your work day?

Messenger: We work seven days and we do not have a limit on how many hours we will work. Sometimes we work up until 11 or 12 o'clock at night. Our work has now become so enormous on us we hardly let go. When we go to sleep or to bed, we just have it to do.

Question: Will you spend your entire winter here?

Messenger: For the last few years I have been spending the whole winter and summer in Chicago.
Question: Have you been going to Phoenix in recent years?

Messenger: No, I have not been to Phoenix in recent years.

Question: If you could pick one overriding issue by which you could be remembered by history, what would it be? What would you want to be remembered for, a century from now?

Messenger: I would only want to be remembered for the work that I do, in the Name of Allah. That is what I want to be remembered for.[14]

The Politics of Succession

Question: Have you designated a successor for yourself?

---

[14] Ibid.

Messenger: I do not do that. I cannot do that. I did not choose myself. God chose me and if He wants a successor, He will choose that one.

Question: By what means would someone come up?

Messenger: I do not know that, because I do not believe there is one coming up. The work that I am doing, I don't think God needs one, because when man and God have come face to face, as the old saying goes, then that is the end of it. When we are face to face with God, that is the end of it and so what would another one do? There is nothing for him to do.

Question: After you are gone, Mr. Muhammad, the Nation of Islam will continue to exist but how?

Messenger: It will be a New Islam to what the old Orthodox Islam is, today. It will be altogether a New One.

Question: You mean your successor will preside over a New Islam?

Messenger: There will be no successor. There is no need for a successor when a man has got the Divine truth and has brought you face to face with God.

Question: How will your resources be administered?

Messenger: That will be carried on by the Nation. After setting up the Nation on the right way, or right path, to take care of themselves, they do not need any more instruction on that. They will follow it as the Constitution of America has been followed.

Question: Will it be run by local Mosques?

Messenger: No, No, No. After this, the whole entire Nation of Black people will be governed Divinely and the government will be a Divine government and not something that is governed locally, like we have today.

We will have a Divine government set up for us, and it will stand forever. We will not need any change.

Question: What did you mean, "new different from Orthodox?"

Messenger: I meant just that. We have a New Islam coming up. The Old Islam was led by white people, white Muslims, but this one will not be. This Islam will be established and led by Black Muslims, only.[15]

---

[15] Ibid.

The Devil In Person

Blue Eyes Only?

Question: The press states that you label all white people blue eyed devils. Is this true?

Messenger: Whether they are actually blue eyed or not, if they are actually one of the members of that race, they are devils.

Will All Devils Be Destroyed?

Question: What would be an out for me? Is there any hope for me?

Messenger: Now, I must tell you the truth. There will be no such thing as elimination of all white people from the earth, at the present time or at the break out of the Holy War. No, because there are some white people today who have faith in Allah and Islam though they are white, and their faith is given credit.

They are not born or created Muslims, but they have faith in what the Muslims are and trying to live. It is only through Islam that white people can be saved. But you see there would be a Holy War (they call it a Holy War which means right is against wrong and wrong against right).

Question: You do not mean whites fighting Blacks or that sort of thing?

Messenger: I do not say I should say "no" because the right is the Black and the wrong is the white, and naturally the Muslim world is bound to clash with the unrighteous world.

Question: Do you mean through guns and that sort of violence?

Messenger: I see a lot of them have been prepared. I do not know what you are going to use, but I know there are lots of weapons prepared. But we are not to use carnal weapons, which you will use. We do not need it. And the sun shining on your back, we can use that, if necessary, for weapons. God Has every kind of weapon out there to use against you, even to the earth you are sitting on. If He Shakes that for a half a minute, all of your cities could lie sprawled.

There is no such thing as Him Preparing the kind of weapons you are preparing. You cannot win in anything. You cannot stop the snow and cold weather from blowing down from the Northwest. There are mountains of it lying there, waiting for a certain time. We cannot do anything against the forces of nature. We have no defense and it is written in the Bible that He Keeps this thing stored away for the day of battle and war, to fight you with. And we cannot do anything about that. There are storms also. Who is it out there who feels so brave with a twister out there tearing up houses on both sides?

Question: You do not feel that members of the Nation of Islam will have to take up guns?

Messenger: No, they would not have to do that, if they obey Allah, anymore than, I would say, Moses and Aaron had to take up arms against Pharaoh.

You have been fighting us with guns and what not, ever since John Hawkins brought us here, over four hundred years ago. We have to find something more effective and the most effective are the forces of nature.[16]

The Natures of Black & White

Question: You mentioned that Black people were born, I believe you said pure?

Messenger: They were born righteous.

Question: And the slave owners made them unrighteous?

Messenger: Yes, they were, by nature, made unrighteous. Their nature was that.

Question: Does that include all white people now?

Messenger: That included all white people then and all white people now. They were made unrighteous.

---

[16] Ibid.

It has been very well lined up to us; we find here in Genesis the making of the man that started trouble. Even his sons started trouble. When they got old enough they started murdering each other and it has kept going ever since, because white people kill white people. They go to war with each other.

They stay at war with each other. According to history, they had a thirty year war in England and a hundred year war in Europe and I see in the paper over here and on the radio, that they are fighting over there, one another, now. They are even fighting the church over there in Ireland. They cannot get at peace with each other, there is the area where they fought the thirty and one hundred year wars.[17]

What's In A Name

Question: In your teachings today, you indicated that we as Black people should get rid of the names that the slave master has given to us over the years. Do you recognize the legality and legitimacy of non Christian names assumed by black people by virtue of court decrees, which names have not been given to the black brothers or sisters by yourself?

Messenger: I recognize any black man's name if he has some kind of origin for it, but I know that if you'll see the hereafter, which means [after] the destruction of this world and names of the devil. [You] will have to have an honorable name that will

---

[17] Ibid.

live and be respected and admired by every one of your people, but the names of the devils of this world, will be destroyed with them. You won't have their name around here to go in. Their language will be destroyed. You won't be able to speak their language, so Allah taught me, after 20 years of destruction of them. You will have to speak your own Holy language, because no one will talk to you in any other language.[18]

Question: Sir, you said something about that you would have to go and have one of God's names. I noticed that friends of mine started naming their children certain Asian names. I would like you to clear that up.

Messenger: You and all your children can be named at once and that's what you can get. I can name you, He's not going to take the name away that I give, but I don't want to be so smart to take over the naming of the people. I do know His names and that's the names that you have to be named in, but I expect Him here pretty soon and I don't want Him to come and find me taking over His job.[19]

Yakub's Time

Question: Mr. Muhammad I would like to know why was Yakub allowed to rule for six thousand years?

---

[18] Theology of Time Audio, October 15, 1972
[19] Theology of Time Audio, September 24, 1972

Messenger: There was no God in his time that could prevent him, and it was necessary for us to learn from one that was in us, in our midst, what he had that could rule others for six thousand years from 9,000 to 15,000.[20]

---

[20] Theology of Time Audio, August 27, 1972

Moon & Planets

Devil In Space

Question: Can you tell me why is the white man going into outer space and how far will he get?

Messenger: Going up in space. It is to fulfill the scripture that thou may ascend up to heaven, above the clouds, but yet I will bring you down to hell.[21]

Spiritual Meaning of The Moon

Question: Is it true that the devil has reached the moon?

Messenger: Why certainly, in a physical way, yes, according to their reports and their pictures on the moon.

Question: [What about the spiritual part?]

Messenger: He has not reached that part, that part that we preach of equality. That's spiritual teaching. And that he has not reached the spiritual equality. That's what we represents the moon for: Equality between man and man; therefore, that moon have not as yet been reached by the devil.

Question: Dear Holy Apostle, from the teachings that I have heard, you have said that the moon

---

[21] Theology of Time Audio, August 27, 1972

represents, as it is right now in the first quarter, the original black people; am I right sir?

Messenger: No, it don't say really "represent" the black man in the stage he's in now, the way you see, but it represents the sign of the Black people that is here in North America that is blind, deaf and dumb and dead to the knowledge of self, but was once in the knowledge of self.

Question: What does the other three quarters represent?

Messenger: It represents stages in our rise into the knowledge of self.[22]

Blacks On Other Planets

Question: Since Black man is the original man, are there black men in among other beings on other planets?

Messenger: I didn't get the teachings of the knowledge of what was on other planets from Him, as He was trying to acquaint me into the knowledge of myself who is on this planet and others who are on this planet.[23]

---

[22] Theology of Time Audio, October 15, 1972
[23] Ibid.

Life After Death

Understand Heaven and Hell

Question: I would like to know if the Nation of Islam teaches of a heaven and hell as in Christianity.

Messenger: No. Not like Christianity, but it teaches of a heaven and hell, but not in the same way that Christianity teaches. We teach of a heaven and a hell while you live.

You cannot be tormented in hell if you are not alive. You got to be alive to feel the torment and if you are in a heaven you got to be alive to feel the joys of heaven.

Question: Then Sir, there is no such thing as life after death.

Messenger: No, if you are referring to a physical death. A physical death does not carry any life, it's physically dead. But if you are referring to a spiritual death, that is true; being dead to the spirit of God, you won't have His spirit in you. [We] then call you dead.

Question: I read in the Bible that man will destroy himself, do you believe that?

Messenger: Yes. I believe it.

Question: In what way?

Messenger: In whatever way you build your life up. You don't have no, nothing out here that will destroy you just because that it can destroy you only when you go to fight each other, but there is nothing prepared out here to destroy you, you destroys yourself, so Allah taught me.

All Life Will Suffer Death

Question: According to the Christian teachings, all men must die, but those who are on the right side of God will go on to an eternal life?

Messenger: Yes, and that's why we are here today, because those on the right side mean those who believe in God and they put their trust in God, and we are defenders of those righteous people.

Question: Do we have to suffer death?

Messenger: There is not a life made, according to the teachings of God to me that will not face death.[24]

---

[24] Ibid.

Prophets & Significant Others

Abraham and Sarah

Question: I wanted to ask you of Abraham. He had a wife by the name of Sarah?

Messenger: Yes Sir.

Question: I wanted to know, was Sarah a white woman?

Messenger: Really brother, I don't know whether she was white of black, but I believe Abraham had every great love for Black, and maybe he had a black wife. If Sarah was white or black, her husband was a great prophet, and the time that we are now in was revealed to him and his prophecy mostly was on the base of us and our return to our own. I don't say that she was white and I don't say she was black, because the Arabs ruling were white. [We] take away the history of us surrounding Abraham, which is true. We are following and fulfilling that which was prophesied by him and whether Sarah was white or black has never been much concern to me, because I wasn't following up on Sarah for any particular prophetic saying in order to bring out some truth here. Only our women have who are sitting under the guidance into righteousness. We use Sarah as a very good woman that they could take pattern after. This is [the] only reason we bring [up] her history.[25]

The True History of Jesus

Question: In regards to the history of Jesus.

Messenger: I want to give you his whole history, as God gave it to me, but I don't have time now. I can say this according to that which you can read: The Holy Qur'an does not call him a God. He was not a God and he had mentioned in the Bible that he came before time to do his type of teaching, and he also admits it in the Holy Qur'an.

It was not the time of the Jews; their time was not up to have judgment teachings taught among them, because they had yet time to live; therefore they cut him off like they did many righteous prophets [so] he couldn't set the world in righteousness [while] they lived under wickedness [to] deceive us and make us do the same....

He was not sent to us at all. Jesus was sent to the Jews, or rather, taken himself to the Jews. There is no prophecy in the Bible that [says] Jesus was to come to preach salvation to the Jews, because he was 2000 years ahead of their time. There's much more we can say, but I think we would be losing time. He admits himself that he was ahead of time, and he prophesied of another one, [when he said], "when He comes, He will teach you and lead you into all truths. I can't do it. I'm sent or I'm here for

---

[25] Theology of Time Audio, June 18, 1972

a special thing, but that One will tell you all." Like the one that Moses prophesied of.

I [Jesus] bear witness with Moses and his words and his teachings, that, "That one will lead you into all truths, I can't do it."

So I think it is very good that we are living in this time, and a time that we learn the truth of that which prophets before us couldn't look into.

Now the book tells you when He comes, whom the God will send. That is he [the One Jesus and Moses referred to], and you will hear from him that which you have been longing for. THIS [Elijah Muhammad speaking of himself] IS HIM, brother (in soft words).[26]

IMPORTANT NOTE: It is critical we put an important note here because the Messenger would use literary devices on many occasions when he speaks. He will take on what's called the third party to speak as though he is personifying the person he is talking for, like he is using their words. An example of this is in the previous dialogue of him using Jesus' words to sound like it was actually Jesus himself speaking.

There are people who will take this manner of public speaking and assert that the Messenger is speaking for himself and therefore is referring to someone else similarly as the person he is speaking for. This is done by the perpetuators to mislead

---

[26] Theology of Time Audio, June 11, 1972

you into thinking that the Messenger is foretelling of them instead of himself.

Mary, Joseph And Siblings

Question: Did Joseph and Mary have another child after Jesus?

Messenger: We find here in the New Testament where they were inquiring of Jesus while he was teaching that someone told Jesus that his mother, brothers and sisters were out there inquiring and the Jesus made it clear that none could be his mother, nor brother or sister unless they believed like him.

This showed that his mother and his brothers was not disbelievers in him if he turned them down like that. He said, these are mine that stand here, meaning those who were on the inside with him. That is true. And the way of the believer: you can't be the brother of the believer or sister of the believer unless you believe like them.[27]

---

[27] Theology of Time Audio, October 15, 1972

The Promised Land

Lost Books of The Bible

Question: I would like to know the authenticity of the lost 10 books of the Bible.

Messenger: I don't know brother. He [Allah] didn't teach me that any books were lost?

Question: According the Bible it teaches that God is a spirit and that was the main thing that kind of [made me] stumble when I first heard your teaching. [Have] these quotes in the Bible been added and how long have this teaching been going on?

Messenger: Ever since the writers of the Book.[28]

The Land of The Wicked

Question: I was reading in the Muhammad Speaks that you were going to come back to the Temple and reveal where the Promise Land was, and I was following the Muhammad Speaks and have not seen you reveal that and I want to know if you still intend to?

Messenger: The place where you are in now. As you may read in the Bible where the Jesus said, that it is the Lord's own good Will to give thee the kingdom. This means a kingdom that you will have

---

[28] Ibid.

to inherit, that is not present at that time, but the kingdom of heaven that's formed for the righteous. And it will be this place that He will give: the kingdom of the wicked.   As Isaiah and other prophets prophesy, that He gives to us the kingdom of the wicked.[29]

Drowning At The Red Sea

Question: The event surrounding Pharaoh, could you tell me if that was a parable, or did that actually happen   The drowning in the Red Sea?

Messenger: Yes. There were signs and events that took place in the time of Pharaoh and his people and Israel was signs of what you see going on today. I don't know what signs you are referring to, but all the history that I have read of Pharaoh and his people with Israel is referring to us and our modern Pharaoh, according to what Allah has taught me.

Pharaoh: Black or White

Question: Was Pharaoh a black man or a white man?

Messenger: No. He was not white; there was not any Egyptian that was actually white at that time, according to the teachings of the history of pharaoh and his people. He was not really white people, because the origin of the population of Egypt was not made white. They were of the original.[30]

---

[29] Ibid.

The Orthodox World
Build The Pyramids

Question: How is it that the Egyptians got the pyramids as high as they did and with what instruments?

Messenger: The Saviour taught me that they had an hydraulic they used in those days that they don't have in use now, and will not put it in use, because the devil will grasp that knowledge. [The devil] doesn't know it yet. He has been asking the question himself. He (Saviour) said to me, he would put that same hydraulic in effect as soon as they remove the devil. They don't want him to know.[31]

Egyptians Blood Mixing

Question: What made the Egyptians wicked?

Messenger: There was in their time the wicked man coming among them 6000 years ago. The wicked devil got a chance to visit among the Egyptians; like when England came among the Egyptians. They deceived the Egyptians [into] follow and doing like them. There were the Turkish in Egypt and they put a little of their devil stuff in them under the rule of Pasha.[32]

---

[30] Ibid.
[31] Ibid.
[32] Ibid.

The Orthodox World

Laws Governing Arab World

Question: Mr. Elijah Muhammad, about two years ago I had a cousin who joined with the Muslims and she was an Orthodox Muslim, and she was one of three wives to her husband. I can't understand why the two are so diverse and why aren't they just a whole?

Messenger: I'm not up here to go over the laws of the Islamic world with you if you read these things, you read them. So, I'm not up here to condemn nor take away anything, only to teach you that which Allah have gave me to teach you.

If there's any more of this kind of talk, we're dismissing, because eighteen hundred to two thousand people could talk on the Orthodox Muslim rules of Islam while they don't know it themselves. You have to come to school for such. You have to be schooled into that and not come and [simply] ask questions, because your questions demand more than just a word or two.

It demands a lot of answers to your questions and the people who are not interested in what you are asking will not like me to keep them in here listening to what you have to say until night. It's getting late and the people would like to go home. I don't care to get involved in a lot of Orthodox Muslims rules, regulations and laws of Islam.

We are bringing to you a new Islam. As I tell white people, they ask me sometimes, they say, well, they say those over there don't believe in your teaching. I say, that's natural. This is something new which they never have heard before. It takes time. Nevertheless, we have the key to the whole world of man whether you believe it or not. I have the key and it's written in your book that I have it; that God gave him the key.

Question: Mr. Muhammad, I'm a old time Detroiter, and I remember a long time ago there used to be a Temple on Theodore and Hastings street way back in the twenties, I wanted to know is it the same set up or has it changed since them.

Messenger: We haven't changed Islam, we go into more knowledge of it but we don't change it.[33]

Arab Recognition & Respect Muhammad

Question: I noticed that within a few weeks the white press and the news media are waging a campaign against the Arabs and the Arab Nations trying to get public sympathy for the Israelis. I wonder could this be because the Arab Nations are starting to recognize the Black Muslim Movement here in the U.S.?

Messenger: Yes, I believe those who have knowledge of what kind of work I am doing in America is beginning to recognize it and respect it.

[33] Theology of Time Audio, August 27, 1972

Persecution of The Muslims

I believe that. This is the greatest that has ever happened in our midst since we have been crucified into slavery by the Whiteman. Never a work of this kind has come in his midst that he wasn't able to attack and win. He doesn't even question this work. You go out there and bring all you can see out there. Not a one of them will question me. There is nothing for him to question me on. He knows the truth, but he is not able to [accept] the truth, but he knows it. He gave me credit for teaching the truth, but he is not able to accept the truth, because there is no truth in him.[34]

---

[34] Theology of Time Audio, October 15, 1972

Persecution of The Muslims

Keep The Niggers Down

Question: The Nation of Islam does have considerable holdings and financial assets. There in the South, recently, I forgot whether it was Alabama or Mississippi, there was a lot of "hullabaloo" about not allowing Black Muslims to obtain farmland, due to the number of people trying to cut down on......

Messenger: We have been living in the world that goes like this "Keep the nigger down." And we are not out of it yet. What we are doing today, we are trying to do something for ourselves. Therefore, we go to the farm where there is the place where everyone, if he wants to be successful, can go back to, the earth, and get it from the earth. This is where the white man got it from. He has been successful ever since he has been in the Western Hemisphere. He has raised enough food to supply his brother in Europe and even our Brothers in Africa, [from] right here in America.[35]

Government Persecution Of Muslims

Question: Have you heard anything to the effect that government officials are trying to put pressure

---

[35] Elijah Muhammad Meets The Press, January 14, 1972

on the Black Muslims similar to the pressure that was put on other Black organizations in the past?

Messenger: I have been doing this work for forty years. I have known many groups to rise up since that time and carry into practice what you have in mind. But actually our people in L.A. and New York or any other place, here in Chicago, they have been mistreated right along. They go to prison and the federal penitentiary, as they call it institutions. But, that is all given to us. The trial of the Black Muslims in America must come to pass. We must be tried.[36]

Registered Muslims

Question: Do you have a central registry of all throughout the country?

Messenger: All of them that come up to register, we do have.

Question: Can you give us a number of those you have?

Messenger: They come so fast. Right at this hour they are trying to get to us now, in the Registry of Islam. We never know how many we have. We believe we have quite a few hundred thousand over the country. And they are coming in faster now than ever.

---

[36] Ibid.

Persecution of The Muslims
A "Good" Muslim

Question: What do you mean when you say, "a Good Muslim?"

Messenger: A good Muslim is one who observes and obeys the laws of the Religion of Islam, designed by God, Himself.

Disobedience & Punishment

Question: Does that mean that there are only people, I suppose, people ousted from the religion at times? If someone is found not to obey the laws, they are expelled?

Messenger: We have such punishment if we find you not obeying the laws of the religion of Islam as it is taught to me by God, Himself, and that I put the law out before the world and especially before the world and especially before those who believe, to follow and obey, we put you out of the circle and we give such time as from thirty days to six, nine, or twelve months also one to five years [even up] to seven years.

We have never had to put a man or woman out for seven years. [However] these are the numbers of times that you are to pay for your disobedience.

Question: If you are expelled or suspended are you listed on the registry? Do you have a list if someone is suspended for a period of seven years for not obeying the laws? Would you still have that person listed on your registry?

Messenger: Yes, we have to keep him on there.

Question: So, if the people were members at any time, you would know that.

Messenger: If we consult our registry to find out whether or not any of these people were listed (the name), we will find it. We are still searching. We never stop searching to see if such and such [person] are on our register, just in case, [or] we punish ourselves. We have a punishment, as I just listed to you, for disobedient Muslims and we always checking our registry for such things as a Muslim doing [or] causing trouble.[37]

---

[37] Ibid.

The King's Men

Supreme Captain Raymond Sharrieff

Question: (Referring to the shooting of Theodore Bey and Supreme Captain Raymond Sharrieff): Why do you think someone would be shooting at Mr. Sharrieff and why do you think someone would be shooting at Theodore Bey?

Messenger: I do not know what you have in your heart. I do not have that knowledge. Why would they go shoot at the man? What was he doing to them to cause their anger to raise that high to want to kill an innocent man sitting behind the wall in his own office?[38]

Malcolm X

Question: I think you have spoken about this in the past. Could you give us an assessment of the life of Malcolm?

Messenger: No, I would not lose any time with a man that has been talked and talked about for years. If the people do not have knowledge of him after these many years, I am not going to waste my time with going into Malcolm's history.

I do not have any time to waste with him, as I think everyone knows Malcolm or did know Malcolm and they know Malcolm's dead.

---

[38] Ibid.

He was teaching, according to what I heard, and the people that were there should give a better report than me.[39]

Cassius Clay aka (Muhammad Ali)

Question: Would you tell us the present status of Muhammad Ali (Cassius Clay)?

Messenger: Cassius Clay is a good Believer. I would say the young man is full of sport and he goes along with sport, too, but I think in his heart he wants to be good.

Question: Will he be returned into full membership into the Nation of Islam?

Messenger: There is nothing one would do that cannot be forgiven, if he repents.
Question: Have you set date for when he comes back into full membership?

Messenger: No, he is actually still a good Believer. As far as certain duties or posts as he used to hold, as teaching the Ministry, I do not know when that will take place.[40]

---

[39] Ibid.
[40] Ibid.

Jockeying For Power

Question: Do you feel that it is incorrect to use the term "power struggle" (in reference to recent events)?

Messenger: As I said here some time ago, this thing has been happening for forty years, but I never pay it any attention. It doesn't annoy me, because I know a person of that sort has as yet to learn what really Islam is, here in America. Islam in America is to reclaim our people and part them in their own. This is the Resurrection of our people in America.

Question: Is that struggle more intense now than it was in the past? You say it has been going on for forty years.

Messenger: Well, I do not meet any different with what I met thirty five or forty years ago. They always will be striving to be something of their own but I do not pay them any attention because I know they will never be successful.

Question: Has somebody been caught trying to get their hands in the cookie jar?

Messenger: I do not know of anything like that, because I do not pay any attention to this annoying talk about someone taking over.

I Am Assured by God, Himself and by the Prophets. I am not particular about others who talk just to hear themselves talk. I would say they are just wasting time. In the Last Days (if you will allow me to say this,) in the Last Days, it is plainly written that you will have Elijah to put you on the right way and this man starts way back here, almost in the beginning. He "travels" with you, throughout your Bible.

This man will fulfill that which is written of him. This is the Resurrection I refer to of our Black people in America. And this is the place that they must come up first. They are in the "crossroads" here and the right way has to be pointed out for them to go out. I do not mean to say they go out of America, but out of the evils of America. They were made unrighteous by the slave-masters. They are not even charged with it. You are forgiven everything of evil, on your accepting Islam your Own. That is all God Asks you to do today: go back to your Own. You are forgiven for everything, because all the evil you did in the past, it was not you; it was the slave-master who made you do evil.

Question: Mr. Muhammad, have you increased your security staff in recent months?

Messenger: No, I would never do that, only according to the people that come to us.....But, I always go with the hopes and with the knowledge that God will protect us, if my followers do as I tell them. I never depend on a group of security guards, only in the way of searching the people to see that the people don't enter the meeting with weapons or such things as whiskey, playing cards or gambling material.[41]

The Last Days

41 Ibid.

The Last Days

How To Strengthen Belief

Question: How can I strengthen my belief?

Messenger: Just keep coming here brother.

Question: When the world comes to an end, will Allah turn His back on the people of the East or will He send someone to teach them who the right God is?

Angels & Black Scientists

Messenger: I am teaching you of who the right God is myself. The Bible says that He will send His Angels from the East to gather us from the west.

Question: After the visiting the Temple and listening carefully, how could one could become a Muslim.

Messenger: Believe what I teach you and follow me.[42]

Question: Were the Original Scientist Black?

Messenger: Yes, according to what God taught me. The original ones were black. They have a kind of circle to them themselves, and they all are black.

---

[42] Theology of Time Audio, October 15, 1972

The Last Days

Question: Whether or not the great northern bean should be eaten.

Messenger: We don't go for eating the large size bean, though they may be the navy bean, but we eat the small size of them, that's what He taught me.[43]

Question: You mentioned that the ten thousand (10,000) angels were here in this country, and I wanted to ask, would they be from among the dead?

Messenger: Yes brother, they are here. They are not to be pointed out to people who will point them out like in the days of Sodom and Gomorrah's destruction. There was the Angel there with Lot that was going to do the job, but they couldn't tell the people before the day that they was going to do it, then the people would have tried to kill them before.

The same way it is today. You can't point out the destroyers of the world to no one, or you [would be] pointing them out to the enemy to attack them at once, because they are human beings like you and I, and we can be killed. If we have [the] power to keep you from killing us, well then, we may bring about the total thing before time that the others get right and get ready to go out.

These things are used by, brother, by wise people and not by people who just would like to tempt God

---

43 Ibid.

or tempt His Messenger for just yourself. You got millions of people in America and they may all not be ready, and God wants to save us all, not to do something just to please someone who would like to tempt God. You can't tempt God brother. This is dangerous to try. To satisfy one person and his desire, you can't do that. We have millions here to please, or rather, to try to save and we hope they'll be pleased with our safety.[44]

Mine Is From Above

Question: Why do we now have to go to the devil to get our knowledge as far as science?

Messenger: Well, it is not my and your way. I'm not in that way. I don't go to the devil to get knowledge. If I had went to the devil to get knowledge you would attack me on that knowledge, but since I didn't graduate from college and universities of his, my knowledge is not of the world. All that I teach came from Allah under the Name of Master Fard Muhammad, to Whom praise is due forever. I got nothing out of the schools and colleges and universities of the white man, I have none of them.

Question: But we have to go to the established schools and universities in order to build a Nation.

Messenger: You don't have to go to the universities of the devil to be able to teach the Nation. As I just told you, I didn't go. I never have been. This is why

---

[44] Theology of Time Audio, July 23, 1972

The Last Days

you must have a change. You can't have a change unless you get out of what you are in and get into another civilization. You will have to have the knowledge of how to get in that civilization. So, I teach you something new. It is not out there in this civilization. You can't find a step of it.

Everything that you teach me even from "A" in the kindergarten of this devil's schools have to be changed from that way and that way of understanding of "A" and "B" over here with us. You say, "Well, go ahead and tell me," Oh, well, let's go ahead in the back and write your name on the book.[45]

Two Places of Refuge In Last Days

Question: In the last days of the Lost Found Nation, how will the Muslims survive?

Messenger: That's what God came for: to save us from that which He will permit to destroy our enemies. He has come to separate the Righteous from the wicked and destroy the wicked and save us from the destruction of that that which He is using to destroy the wicked.

Question: Since your teaching on the Theology of Time, approximately ten weeks back, you said that in the destruction of America there were two places of refuge. I was wondering if you could reveal those two places.

---

[45] Theology of Time Audio, October 15, 1972

Messenger: Well, if I did, there are two. I can prove to you there are two. Here is one, number one: [refuge] with you Lord and my Lord. Good question brother.[46]

The following documents and CD Audios on which this book is based can be obtained by visiting, writing or calling the following:

Secretarius MEMPS
111 E Dunlap Ave, Ste 1-217
Phoenix, Arizona 85020-7802
Phone / Fax : 602 466-7347
Email: secmemps@gmail.com
Website: www.memps.com

Free Catalog Available!

---

[46] Ibid.

The Last Days

16269054R00046

Made in the USA
Lexington, KY
15 November 2018